SOUTHSEA

The latest in our series of booklets cove
Southsea. In this book we cover the area
including the common. The streets section
Directory.

The 1904 B.M.A. Conference handbook says:

"Sunny Southsea – so called because of the illustrious office of the day is very much in evidence here. Southsea has made rapid advances in public favour as a watering place. In 1899 when the British Medical Association held its annual meeting in Portsmouth, emphatic testimony was borne by distinguished members of the profession to the salubrity of Southsea. Under the genial stimulus of its breezes from the sea, visitors speedily recover their pristine health and are then able to appreciate its diversified features of interest."

Historical Background

Much of the land at the south of Portsea Island was for a great many years unsuitable for building. A number of springs fed into streams that led south into marshy areas known as morasses. The larger of these marshy areas, the Great Morass, was shaped like a hand with the palm at the south, by South Parade Pier, with four fingers running north. It was filled in and partially drained over many years starting in the 1700s. The actual morass at the south was not filled in until 1831 to 1843. The last of the 'fingers' was known as the Minnow Pond or Craneswater. In 1886 this was formalised and became the Canoe Lake. At least one spring still survives and can be found under the King's Theatre. Another 'finger' used to stretch up to the bottom of Old Fawcett Road, and Waverley Road seems to follow the western bank of the morass. Most of the land was split between two owners, the Leekes and the Whites. They leased it out, most of it was used as small farms and as time went by was sold off as building land. The other marsh known as the Little Morass was at the Clarence Pier end of the common. This was fed by a stream known as the Hambrook, which had its source in Kingston where Lake Road later joined Kingston Road.

Southsea Common was formerly the waste of Froddington Manor and became known as Southsea Common after the building of Southsea Castle at Keat's Point by Henry VIII in 1545. In 1785 the Lord of the Manor of

Froddington sold the common to the Government for military purposes. Convicts drained and levelled it between 1831 and 1843. Clarence Esplanade was constructed in 1847 and is part of the sea defences built to stop the sea encroaching back onto the common. This was all carried out under the instruction of Lord FitzClarence who was commander of the garrison. After the First World War unemployed people were used to gather stones from the common to allow its use for recreation. The common was purchased by the Corporation in 1923 who then spent £60,000 converting it for leisure use. Double avenues of Huntingdon Elms were planted and a vigorous publicity campaign mounted as a counter measure to unemployment.

Because of this the building line in Southsea is a long way back from the seafront. Many of the large houses were built for prominent local business men or service personnel and had accommodation for their household staff. Some of the other buildings were built as hotels or apartments. In recent years some of the hotels have been converted into flats and apartments or homes for the elderly.

Lumps Farm

The farm was part of Milton Manor from 1600 to 1835 and covered just over 43 acres. It was leased to various tenants over the years including Francis Winten (1600-1627), Ralph Lumpee (until 1660), Richard Cotton (until 1690), Thomas White (1690), John Osmond (1785). It was sold to the Government in August 1835. In 1887 Daniel Netley is listed at what is left of the farm.

General Memories of the Area

"My earliest memories were of going to the beach with my parents, uncles, aunties and my cousins. For me as a child it was all very exciting, there seemed to be plenty of sandwiches, squash, tea in flasks and lots and lots of laughter. My family mostly chose halfway between Southsea and Eastney. The beach was wide and there were long stretches of sand and when the tide went out it was marvellous to run in the water and jump the waves. Then of course there was no such thing as sun tan lotion and we all on occasion got very burnt. Then calamine lotion was applied so the children went to bed looking like ghosts! Some weekends it became cold but we stuck it out and put cardigans on and then eventually walked up Henderson Road to Bransbury Park to go on the swings before catching the bus home. This was an all day affair, in the morning the children and mums would put on their costumes with much laughter as towels had to be held around you whilst you changed. The men only removed their jackets and shoes. My Mum and Aunties had knitted bathing costumes, my cousin, Robert, had knitted trunks which became very heavy when wet, all the girls had costumes which were rouched, some even became transparent when wet! After lunch games were played with the adults, one last dip in the water, we all put on our best clothes and had tea.

My older cousins came regularly to Southsea from Birmingham, there were two sisters and a brother. They loved everything about Southsea, the beach, going into the sea on what must have been wooden paddle boats, walking along the promenade to the Rock Gardens and the fair. The sisters loved flirting with the sailors.

As the years went on things slightly changed. My Auntie Florrie and Uncle Charlie thought they would like a beach hut which they had for many years and I know gave them and the family a great deal of pleasure. My Father bought a television and preferred to watch cricket at home in the comfort of an armchair. My Mother still went to the beach with myself and school friends but mostly towards South Parade Pier where the stones seemed larger and it was agony to walk over them into the water.

I do not believe English summers were any better when I was a child but as none of us had been abroad it didn't seem to really matter. It was always a good day out, I went home really tired and didn't want to go to school in the morning."

Margaret Webster

"When we were children, we were all very street wise and although of a tender age there was no part of Portsmouth that we didn't know. From Old Portsmouth to Hilsea we knew every nook and cranny. I can remember when I was fourteen onwards, of a Sunday we used to go to Eastney beach by Fort Cumberland and for 1/6d (7½p) you could hire a tent for the day and if you were early you would get a front row. We used to take a Primus stove, kettle, basins of cockles, tinned fruit and ice-cream, and we had the time of our lives. Along at South Parade Pier was a lovely theatre and ballroom and the end of the pier had a pierrot show. Across the road was the Savoy Ballroom and the lovely Beach Hotel. Further along at Clarence Parade was another ballroom and opposite was the Esplanade Ballroom which had a coloured glass floor. What wonderful times we had, and I don't ever remember a fight or any arguments.

My sister and her husband first opened what is now the Jolly Sailor but was originally the Westfield. I can remember 1945, the Canadian and New Zealand Navies were put up in Lennox Road South and I've seen them do the Maori War Dance on the tables. It used to get packed every day. The Americans were stationed in Burgoyne Road. The Turret was the place for the Merchant Navy and the Pendragon for the WRENS. On V.E. night thousands of people all went bathing in the sea. All the lights in the harbour came on and Southsea was lit up.

Another event I used to go on was a 1/- (5p) trip to the Isle of Wight. We used to catch the paddle steamer at South Parade Pier about 10am and sail right around to Shanklin, and not come back until night."

Mrs. Dorothy Aslett

"I can well remember long rows of bath chairs with their attendants patiently waiting for customers and also the goat carriages and the donkey rides."

"In the very early 1950s my parents took me to what I presume was the Southsea Show of the day. It was held on the Common and I think it was the first postwar show of its kind held in the City. I cannot remember much about it apart from there being a lot of animals (the farm variety) including an enormous white bull, which I photographed with my new Ensign 'Clear Vue' camera. This produced a 2" square print which is still in existence somewhere in the family archives. I associate the show as having more in common with the big country shows of today rather than the type of show that now graces our common on an annual basis.

Around 1960 when doing a two year stint in the Tudor Crescent, Cosham, T.A. (457 Wessex HA.RA.TA), I was asked or rather told that I along with other 'Weekend Soldiers' would be taking part in an important parade at the Victoria Barracks in Southsea. As one of I think, three Don Rs (Dispatch Riders) I would be lined up with many more of the Cities' Territorials to be inspected by none other than 'Monty' (Field Marshal The Lord Montgomery of Alamein to give him his full title) All the 'Bull' associated with the army was in operation from polishing buttons to polishing motorbikes. Our unit had two BSA 500cc sidevalves and one 350cc OHV Matchless all of which had seen better days.

We arrived on cue, lined up and waited. At last the great man arrived and just walked past the lines of assembled khaki not appearing to take any notice of anyone at least until he reached yours truly. He stopped, looked and uttered words which have no doubt been directed many times at many a more worthy soldier than myself. "Your hat's not straight lad!" and walked on. At the time I did not bother myself too much with this distinction but as time went on it dawned that the Nation's hero of WWII had actually spoken to me!"

Malcolm Garlick

Alhambra Road named after the Spanish palace near Granada.

"During the war I worked in the Mandalay Cafe, in Alhambra Road where the majority of the customers were locally stationed soldiers, with sailors from HMS Collingwood. Unfortunately it was bombed and then moved to Clarendon Road"

Mrs. Williams (née Bone)

West Side

4	Alhambra Private Residential Hotel, Mrs. Martin
8	Private Hotel, Mrs. Emily Binning
12-14	Wellington House Private Hotel, Mrs. J. Hall
18	Harold Ripper, Teacher of Elocution

East Side

3	Private Hotel, Miss E. Reynolds
3	Miss E Reynolds, Lamp Shade Maker
9	Ivydene Boarding Establishment, Mrs. C. Bailey
11	Surrey Private Hotel, A. H. Hill

Beach Road, presumably because it is near the beach.

North Side

2	Beach View Boarding Establishment, Miss W. Hunt

South Side

	John Bowley, Haulage Contractor
9	Arthur Flawn, Accountant
33	Miss Mary Truscott, S.R.N. Nurse
	T. Littlewood, Motor Garage

Bellevue Terrace was commenced in 1809 and completed in 1815. The houses were built piecemeal and have been rebuilt or re-fronted over the years. When the fortifications of Old Portsmouth were opposite it would have had a 'Good View'.

> 5   Has Fleur De Lys railings.
>
> 7   At the rear there is a fine bow window.
>
> 9   George Tee, Confectioner
>
> 12   Restored in 1977 after a fire.

Kings Rooms

> The name was transferred from the elegant pump room, baths and reading room built in 1865 where Clarence Pier now stands to the ballroom of the Royal Pier Hotel.

Royal Pier Hotel

> The site was first occupied by the Bugle Inn. This was demolished and the Pier Hotel built in 1862 or 1865 depending which reference book you believe. By 1898 it had been prefixed Royal. The building closed in 1939 and was used by the WRENS, from 1945 it was used a transit residence by the MOD, later becoming Weston Naval Hotel. It closed in 1966 and was then purchased by Portsmouth Polytechnic in 1969 and used as student accommodation and was from 1973 to 1995 known as Rees Hall. The building has now been demolished and has rebuilt as a new student accommodation block which externally resembles the old building.

The Royal Albert Yacht Club

> formed in 1878 in memory of Prince Albert had its headquarters in the hotel, see also Clarence Parade.

Clarence Esplanade

> Esplanade Assembly Dance Rooms, H & L Dike
>
> Esplanade Hotel, Harry Padbury
>
>> Built in 1877. It was a wooden structure so that in the event of any conflict it could be quickly dismantled to allow the guns on the fortifications to fire out to sea. This of course did not occur but the building was a casualty of the second world war when it was bombed along with the pier.
>
> Esplanade Assembly Rooms Cafe, H & L Dike
>
> The Assembly Rooms, 6 flats

William Tarring in his memories (deposited at the City Record Office) says of the Battle of Southsea:

> "When the Esplanade Hotel was built the Company tried a bit of cribbing by enclosing the piece of beach in front and connecting it up with the pier, a number of local men were mixed up in the attempt which caused great excitement and a riot ensued, which has facetiously been termed 'The battle of Southsea'. A barricade was erected across from the Hotel to the Pier which the people promptly pulled down and the police were called upon. That's where the mischief was done if they had contented themselves with just keeping the people moving, but instead of which a cordon of police was drawn across the opening thus denying right of way which the people resented. Stones were thrown and the police made a baton charge, and attacked everyone indiscriminately. People like myself were attracted there just out of curiosity but taking no active part. I stood close to a fat sergeant and was just about to ask him what it was all about when I felt his truncheon on my head and I was clutching at his belt. Just at that moment I saw more stars, than ever there were in the firmament. I returned and rejoined my van and went on my rounds. I afterwards, foolishly perhaps, resolved to return and demand an explanation. In the meantime, I suppose, the police had been roughly handled and had got infuriated. I had only got halfway across the Common and was standing quietly under a lamp when the rush came and I had my head laid open, the blood streaming down my back. If I could have laid my hand on a missile or weapon I fear I might have embroiled myself by a reprisal, instead of which I went to the residence of Mr. Parson on Kings Terrace. He was Chairman of the Pier Company, so he was discretely 'not at home', so I went home and wrote him a letter which brought him out to Portsea before we had finished breakfast. When he tried to soap me over and was profuse in regrets assuring me to his innocence in the matter, which I took 'Frans cum salis'. I then wrote to the Mayor who called a public meeting and I advertised for witnesses, but a very few came forward and those who did were halfhearted about it. Having related my experience I was asked who it was who gave the order to charge, but I was not able to be caught in that way not being absolutely certain

although I felt sure it was the man who stood by my side, viz Richard Barber, Superintendent of Police. When I had finished the Mayor asked him, what he had to say about my evidence. His reply was "I cannot dispute anything Tarring has said Sir". What was the opinion of the Watch Committee was not divulged except that they thought I was indiscreet in returning as I did, but the fact remained that the cause was won and the right of way was maintained. I was a Bête Noire to Richard Barber forever after. I have reason to believe that he had a dressing down over it.

Sometime after I was present in a Company which included Johnnie Howell a blatant demagogue, who was always kicking up a fuss and George Cunningham the blonde Counsellor. The conversation (in which I took part) related to Barber "I tell you what it is John" said Cunningham "the fact Barber is like you, he lacks discretion". That sums up the whole matter. It was Barbers indiscretion that caused the Battle of Southsea."

Clarence Esplanade Pier (Southsea Clarence Esplanade Pier Co. Ltd.)

Clarence Pier

Southsea Pier as it was first known was built in 1861 and opened on the 1 June 1861. A tram car service linked the pier to the town station at Landport and ships departed for the Isle of Wight. The pier was extended in 1874 and in August 1882 the new pavilion was opened by the Prince and Princess of Wales. It has been renamed during this period Clarence to avoid any confusion with the new pier that was built at South Parade. The pier was extensively damaged in the war and the pier buildings were finally rebuilt and opened on 1 June 1961 at a cost of £400,000.

Kimbell's Cafe

Thomas Hill, Bookseller

Goodie's Cafe (Southsea) Ltd., Confectioners

William Butlin, Amusement Caterer.

Remembered by most people as Mannings, but William Butlin is listed from 1934 to 1962. Billy Manning is only listed from 1964 to 1976 when the directories stop.

"The area alongside the pier and later the site of the Esplanade Hotel were used as a Funfair and Amusement Arcade. William (Billy) Butlin, later the Manning's and then the Shufflebottoms had the main concession on the fair. During Manning's days there were some old rides, like the Carousel Roundabout and Helter Skelter – these were not run down but beautifully painted and kept in good order. The Carousel which is still on the much reduced site is more than one hundred years old and has recently had a new electric motor system installed. Other attractions were the big wheel, ghost train, dodgems and of course the penny in the slot arcades. On a Saturday visit Mum would play on a game where you rolled an old penny down and tried to get it to land on a striped area without crossing the stripes to win a 1d, 2d or 3d. We would have a go on a game where you dropped ping pong balls in the mouth of a moving goose and tried to get the balls to drop into slots to win a prize – of course you never did! Just like the cranes where you tried to collect a compass or yo-yo or other toy, we never saw anyone succeed on that either. In the road way dividing the funfair was often a man with a small monkey which was dressed in clothes. He would try to make people hold it while he took a photo of them and then you had to pay for the photo. One attraction outside the amusement arcade at Clarence Pier was the laughing sailor, a penny in the slot would result in him moving from side to side and laughter coming from the grilles around the machine. (He can now be found in the City Museum in semi-retirement with only the occasional user). On Sundays if we walked along the seafront from South Parade Pier to Old Portsmouth we would walk through the fairground but were not allowed to stop."

Stephen Pomeroy

"Had its beginnings around 1931 as a small mobile concern run by an amusement caterer by the name of Billy Butlin. Its original site was approximately where the car park on the common now stands. It quickly found its present site and became Funacres. I use the term present site, but in reality it was the area south of the dividing road. The area to the north of the road came later.

The original amusements consisted of a 'Big Dipper', a roundabout reminiscent of Walt's Waltzer of later years and a large arcade area. In the 1950s it rapidly developed to its maximum area and was open all year as opposed to just Easter and summer periods of its early years.

The 'Big Dipper' survived the war and became known as the 'Wild Mouse'. Rumour had it that a sailor once stood up in his car on the top run only to be thrown to his death when the track and the car turned abruptly through 90 degrees. Arguably the most popular ride was Walt's Waltzer. Whether or not this was a re-vamped version of the pre-war ride or of a similar design I do not know. Basically it was an upmarket roundabout for teenagers. I think its popularity was due to the fact that it always played the latest pop music.

Personally I remember many rides to Del Shannon singing 'Runaway' in the early 1960s.

Other 'big' things to go on were the dodgems, ghost-train, big wheel, chair-o-planes, carousel with gallopers (horses that went up and down), Wall of Death with motorcycles, large swing boats known to some, for some reason, as 'Noah's Ark, a large swinging cage, Helter Skelter and the centrifuge or rotor wall. This spun round and you stuck to the wall by centrifugal force.

All of these were surrounded by smaller stalls and slot machines. Stalls remembered were Hoop-La, Air Rifles firing pellets or darts at various targets, coconut shy, fortune teller, roll-a-penny, roll-a-shilling and darts – on a dartboard score below 21 or hit a small linen bag which held an undisclosed sum of money in. You won what was in the bag you hit. Slot machines were many and varied usually at a penny a go. I can only remember one by name and that was the haunted house. Bagatelle and What-the-Butler-Saw were also available but I think the latter cost 6d. Stalls selling candy floss, ice-cream, sweets and doughnuts were also on site, the traditional Hall of Mirrors and believe it or not, what can only be described as a zoo! This was situated right in the north-east corner of the fair alongside the entrance and was probably about 12 feet square. It cost 6d to get in and you squeezed through a narrow gap between the cages. I assume that the cages had glass or perspex fronts to protect both the animals and the public from each other. I think the whole had a corrugated iron roof which must have made it unbearable for the animals during the hot weather. The only animal I can remember was in the last cage as you came out. This was a small monkey which was always doing something unmentionable. I don't think this lasted for long but was around 1960.

The small shops outside the fair were much the same as today and I usually invested in a superb crab roll costing 2/6 each time I went to there. On the corner of Clarence Pier by the entrance to the fair was a small pub in the shape of an Igloo and called the Igloo Bar. The old traditional laughing sailor had pride of place in the entrance to the pier. For the uninitiated this was an animated model of a sailor about 3 feet tall in a glass case. You inserted your 6d and he would then give voice to a really infectious laugh to young and old alike. Fortunately he still survives in the City Museum.

One of the items I remember from the funfair in the 1950s was where you could make your own record. It was similar to a telephone booth and when you got inside you put your money into the slot and either sang or spoke into the microphone on the wall. After so many minutes the machine finished and a disc came out about the size of a 45rpm single record came out. When you got home you put your record on your record player, the quality of the reproduction was terrible.

When Billy Manning was running the fair he actually lived on the site. He had two large caravans parked side by side and joined by a specially made corridor. If you looked down on them they were in the shape of an H. They were parked where the end of the moat now turns north towards Pembroke Road.

When my mum was younger she went for a ride on the big roundabout. Unfortunately at the time her bag was open and a lot of loose change fell out. At the end of the ride she told the attendant who promptly helped her look for it both around and under the ride. They were helped by onlookers and she was convinced that she had got back more money than she had lost in the first place!"

Malcolm Garlick

The references in the trade directory that follow are to the various kiosks and buildings along the seafront.

R. Hodges & Son Ltd., Tobacconist

T. Wall & Sons Ltd., Ice Cream Manufacturers

Speedboat

Harry Davis, Fruiterer
Nearby you could take speed boat trips along the seafront or more sedate trips around the harbour to see the Warships, earlier at the turn of the century donkey rides were available on the common opposite Clarence Pier and goat cart rides along the seafront.

Southsea Rowing Club, Boat House
Mrs. A. Sessions, Refreshments.
A. Adams, Fruiterer
Dagostino's (Mrs. T. Byerley), Ice Cream Merchants
Mrs. L. Halson, Confectioner
Charles Dove, Refreshments.
William Halson, Confectioner
Victor Durrant, Café,
Portsmouth Swimming Club
Founded in 1875 in summer swam in the sea, the remainder of the year at the corporation baths. An annual swimming festival was held August Bank Holiday weekend.
G. Langley, Confectioner.
Charles Hemington, Confectioner

H. Gregory, Confectioner
Life Boat Tea House (City of Portsmouth Corporation)
Royal Albert Yacht Club, Boat House
Children's Corner (City of Portsmouth Corporation)

"A miniature steam railway ran along the seafront behind a low wall. Later it became diesel and then electric. At the Castle end of the ride in the mid-fifties were figures from childrens' stories and nursery rhymes. The Mad Hatter, Humpty Dumpty, gnomes etc., which were sadly vandalised and then removed. Also here were pony rides, a paddling pool and swimming pool – both open air, and a boating lake with small motor boats. The only problem with the motor boats was that the arrow on the front never pointed in the same direction as the steering wheel."

Stephen Pomeroy

"Although for whatever reason our family did not frequent Southsea very much during the 1950s I do remember that on the rare occasions that we did visit my favourite place was where the Sea Life Centre is now. I would have been around ten years old and was mad on model railways. The miniature railway was a natural enlargement of this hobby. The train was real steam and was very popular with children of both sexes and their fathers. There was always a queue to pay but after that you just stood on the platform until the previous occupants had vacated their seats and then jumped on. The engine was in the meantime disconnected and driven onto the turntable where it was turned onto a passing loop line and reconnected at what had been the back end of the train. This in itself was a novelty as most other miniature railways at that time had a continuous loop. It is therefore of some interest to note that the City's other railway at Hilsea also had its own turntable. The Southsea line was about a twelve inch gauge and followed what (if viewed from the air) would have resembled a figure six with a station at the top. About halfway round the loop I think was a tunnel. If memory serves me right this consisted of a war time Anderson Shelter with the ends removed. At about the same place was a short spur line to the engine shed where the engine was kept overnight. I assume the carriages were left in the open. Next to the railway was the boating lake and the swimming pool. I don't think I ever used the latter but from memory it was always fairly crowded. I did sometimes use the boat. I think there was two types on the same stretch of water but separated by some sort of a bar. The very young had hand driven paddle boats while the older ones could go on the speedboats. The term speedboat is a bit of a misnomer. They were certainly of that style with varnished hulls and leather covered seats but that is where the likeness ended. They were electrically driven and I doubt that they moved much faster than the kiddies paddle boats.

The area later went through a series of changes including go-karts. Model cars, and model boats (all aimed at childrens' amusement) and eventually ended up as todays Sea Life Centre"

Malcolm Garlick

Southsea Castle
"This was only visible from the outside as it was still owned by the government and always looked run down and derelict. On the common side were the tea rooms and offices. Later the Castle was sold to the Council who then demolished the tea rooms and offices and converted the Castle into a Museum. The floral clock was in front of the tea rooms."

"The Floral Clock was in the first place round about where the forecourt is of the Pyramids and alongside was a small rock garden. When Southsea Castle Gardens were being constructed round about 1964-1965 it was decided to move the Floral Clock so that it would become the focal point of Castle Avenue and a foreground to the Southsea Castle Gardens, which I designed

Floral Clock and Tea Rooms

when I was a technical assistant. Smiths, the famous clock manufacturers presented the original clock mechanism to the city and there was a plaque, which dedicated the clock to the citizens of Portsmouth for their bravery during the Second World War."

Brian Kidd

Southsea Beach & Publicity Committee (City of Portsmouth),
    Enquiry Office and Ice Cream Shop.
Southsea Castle Tea House (City of Portsmouth Corporation)
Sports Pavilion, Southsea Common

Clarence Parade
    The Queens Hotel stood on the corner with Osborne Road. Built originally as Southsea House it burnt out in 1901. In 1904 it was rebuilt to design of architect T. Cutler, at first only the western half, the remainder added later.

1-2	Gladstone Hotel, C. Mutty
1-2	Gladstone & Carlton Hotels Ltd., Registered Office

here is Auckland Road West

8	James Bringan, Ophthalmic Surgeon. From 1884 to his death in 1907 was the home of Lieut., later Rear-Admiral James Raby V.C. He won the V.C. for his actions at Sebastapol. His grave is in Highland Road Cemetery.
15	Elliot Bird and Ronald McHardy, Physicians and Radiologists.
18	Harry Farncombe, Physician
20	Edward Taylor, Physician
26	Palmerston House Private Hotel, Miss I. Summer

here is Palmerston Road

	Hamilton House Private Hotel, Mr. & Mrs. H. Whiteside
27	Alington House Private Hotel, Mrs. G. Chinn
29	Thurlow Mansions, 7 flats
29B	Courtlands Private Hotel
29C	Miss Muriel Wright, Swedish Massage and Radiant Heat Treatment.
	Parade Hotel From 1851 to 1859 the Castle Tavern, was at St. Helens View,

by 1865 the address had changed to Clarence Parade, in 1879 number 27 and 1887 number 29. It was rebuilt in 1897 and the name changed to the Parade Hotel. It was a Tessier's brewery house.

37   Regency Private Hotel, Maj. A. Knox-Gore
38-39 Glenlyon Hotel Ltd.
42   Clarence Hall Private Hotel, Mrs. Welfare
44   Balmoral Hall Private Hotel, Mrs. E. McCausland
48-51 Eversfield Private Hotel, D. Heaword
54   Westfield, 6 flats
           In 1946 the Westfield flats were taken over and was listed as a beer retailer. By 1948 it is named The Jolly Sailor.

here is Lennox Road South

56-60 Pendragon Private Hotel
61   Red Lodge, 4 flats
62   Royal Portsmouth Corinthian Yacht Club.
Lennox Mansions, 2 houses and a hotel.
The Turret Private Hotel, B. Prince

Clifton Road was earlier known as Mill Lane after the Windmill which was on the site.

West Side

Royal Naval Maternity Home, Miss A. Richards, matron
Royal Albert Yacht Club
           The club headquarters were sold by auction on 23rd March 1938 having been the headquarters for sixty years.
           Facilities enjoyed by the members included: dining room, smoking room, two billiard rooms, three card rooms, writing room, six bedrooms plus accommodation for the staff.
Clifton Terrace – 6 houses

Eastern Parade was earlier known as Lumps Lane, then Lumps Road named after Lumps Farm and its former owner Ralph Lumpee.
South Side

Canoe Lake

> Known originally as Craneswater or the Minnow Pond, alongside it stood Lumps Mill which was pulled down in March 1881. The last owner of the Mill was J. B. Eltham. In 1884 the pond was strewn with rubbish. In 1884 the Borough Engineer, Mr. Percy Boulnois designed a scheme for making the Canoe Lake at a cost of £1,900. The pond was excavated to a depth of 2 feet 6 inches and two culverts for the supply of seawater. The paths around the new lake were proposed to be used for cycle racing. The Lake was completed and opened by Mayor Alderman A. S. Blake on June 17, 1886.
>
> "Home to many swans and during the season rowing boats, canoes and pedal boats. These were not like the pedal boats there now, but wooden ones with a handle on each side. Alongside the lake was a childrens' playground with pedal cars, see-saws and swings. Nearby was the Model Village and the Rose Gardens both converted from Lumps Fort."

Cumberland House.

> In 1928 Cumberland Lodge was purchased by Alderman A. E. Porter who then transferred it to the Corporation for the price he had paid, £5,200. In 1932 it was fitted out as an Art Gallery and Natural History Museum. It was originally the commanding officers house for the Marine Barracks. To its south-east was Lumps Fort.

Lumps Fort

> In 1931 when no longer required by the War Office it was put up for sale. In 1932 after negotiations the Corporation bought the site for £25,000. Up until the war various schemes were proposed to develop the fort, but it was not until after the war that any plans were made. Then all the grand schemes were abandoned and in 1950 part of the fort handed over to the Parks department to become the Rose Garden. The remainder was leased to a Mr. Pearson who planned to open a zoo and aquarium. In 1956 Mr. J. C. Simmonds was constructing his model village on the site.

"On holidays the beach was the place to go, stopping there and back for a drink from the metal cups chained to the base of the Emanuel Fountain in the

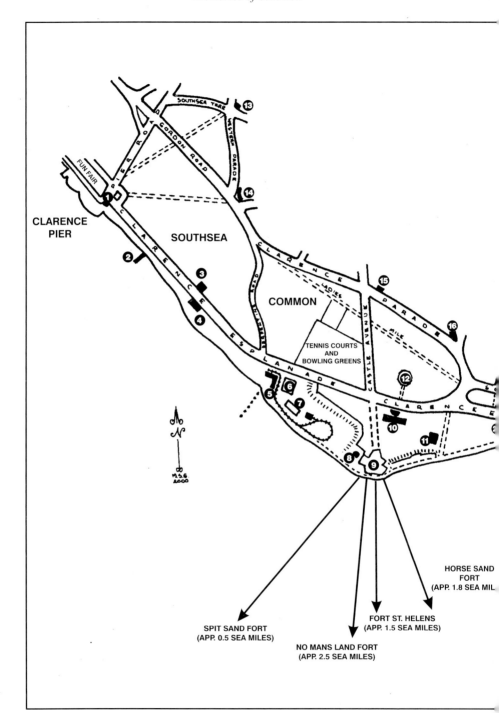

MAP REFERENCES

1. IGLOO BAR c.1962
2. SPEEDBOAT PONTOON
3. R.N. MEMORIAL 1929
4. LIFEBOAT STATION 1886 - 1918
5. MODEL RAILWAY 1932
6. BOATING LAKE
7. SWIMMING POOL
8. LIGHTHOUSE 1820s
9. SOUTHSEA CASTLE 1539
10. CAFE & FLORAL CLOCK
11. ROCK GARDENS PAVILION 1947
12. BANDSTAND c.1922
13. WHEELBARROW PH
14. CRICKETERS PH
15. PARADE HOTEL PH
16. JOLLY SAILOR PH
17. CUMBERLAND HOUSE 1928
18. MODEL VILLAGE 1952
19. LUMPS MILL c.1809
20. ROCK GARDENS 1932
21. CANOE LAKE (SEE OVER)
22. CLARENCE PIER 1861
23. CANOE LAKE APPEARS TO HAVE STARTED AROUND 1866

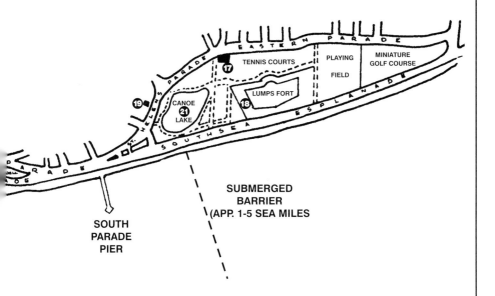

SOUTHSEA SEA FRONT

Canoe Lake. On wet days Cumberland House Museum was a favourite haunt until we were asked to leave. So onto the Rock Gardens to watch and tease the caged birds when the sun came out."

Alan Keel

Canoe Lake

"The City Museum was here for many years, a traditional old fashioned museum with all the exhibits from natural history to art and furniture all fitted into the old house. The only other museum was Charles Dicken's birthplace in Commercial Road."

North Side

On the corner with Festing Grove were Redlands, three flats.

here is Helena, Bruce and Spencer Roads
Eastman's School Playing Ground

here is Cousins and Burbidge Groves

Branksome House – 3 flats
33   John Pink J.P.

here is Brading Avenue

Alfred Aaron Jacobs, one of the developers of Craneswater, he was a house furnisher with a large shop at North End.
43   George Smith, Architect who was responsible for amongst others South Parade Pier and the Municipal College.
47   Major Sir William Dupree, Baronet and head of Portsmouth and Brighton United Breweries.

Jubilee Terrace Commenced in 1809 it was completed in 1827 and named after the Golden Jubilee of George III
1   Homestead Garages (M. Cobb), Motor Cycle Dealers
2   H. Shepherd, Estate Agent
14   Was built in c1809 and still retains the bow windows and railings that were added by the Victorians.
15   Jubilee Tavern, Edward Saunders
      It is first mentioned in the trade directories as a pub in 1867 it was a Lush's brewery house.

King's Terrace
Originally the terrace was symmetrical and was built in 1810 by John Williams, Comptroller of Customs in honour of King George.
Princes House 1926.
      The carved beaver over the door is the symbol of the Alliance Building Society. This was the first branch office of the former Brighton & Sussex Building Society established in 1863. The six coal hole covers in the pavement mark the positions of six earlier houses.
"I remember Southsea when I went to my first job. It was as a temporary filing clerk at the Inland Revenue. The dreaded income tax people used part of Prince's House with Abbey National. I used to get off the bus at Coronation House to walk along King's Terrace. This was 1948 and although the war was over there were several gaps where buildings had been demolished. Prince's House is a cream four storey square building with a flat roof. I ventured up

there once with a friend to see the fine view. This friend was William Jenkins. He had been there in the war. Once when he was fire watching, he told me he had run around the parapet. The threat of being killed in the air raid gave him the idea. I enjoyed the job because it was easy. People walked about talking, smoking, drinking tea at times. The sense of freedom amazed me. I was at my desk one day when an old man asked me to cut down on my whistling. He explained very kindly how it kept him awake! I never knew his name but I remember his diplomacy. My mother worked on the top floor with some other ladies cooking dinners. She was assured that I had a proper dinner until we met again at home."

Anton Cox

South Parade
Lennox Mansions, seven flats.
4   Stanley Hillman, Consulting Surgeon.

here is Florence Road

11   Young Women's Christian Association Hostel & Club, Miss
         L. Woolcott, Warden.
15-17 Solent Private Hotel, Miss F. Baker
18   Slatter's Commercial Hotel, H. Slatter
19   Arundel Private Hotel, Mrs. A. Hill
20   Gill Spencer, Private Hotel
22   Sandon Private Hotel, W & K Cheesman
23   Glendower Private Hotel
24-25 Highcroft (Private) Hotel Ltd.
27A   The Burgoyne Cafe. G. Jones & H. Mitchell

here is Burgoyne Road

28   Eastman's Preparatory School for Boys, E. Singleton & T. Drought.
         They prepared boys for entry into the services.
29   Netley Mansions, eight flats

here is Eastern Villas Road

Strathearn Private Residential Hotel, G. O'Rorke

here is Kirkstall Road

37A   Services Children's Home for Orphans, Matron Miss L. Crewe
38   Redendene Private Hotel, Mrs. J. Reade
41   Fleet House, Boarding House and Cafe (Mrs. E. Stark)
     Later the Esplanade Hotel. Opened in 1942 following the bombing of the original which was alongside Clarence Pier. It was renamed Fanshawes in 1983 and since then the bars have had various names.
42   Inglenook Cafe & Tea Rooms, Mrs. Halladey

here is Clarendon Road

Savoy Garage (Haig's Motors Ltd.)
     Savoy Buildings occupy the site of the former coastguard cottages
     "In the basement of Savoy buildings was Southsea Aquarium and Chipperfield's Chimps. The aquarium was mostly local cold water fish but they did have some tropical fish and a large turtle – Tiny."
1   Robert Waite, Tobacconist.
2   The Savoy Cafe (The Savoy & Mikado Cafes (Southsea) Ltd.)
3   Funland, Edmonds & Davis, Amusement Caterers
4   Mrs. Elizabeth Morley, Confectioner.
5   J. B. Skelton & Co., Auctioneers.
6   Geoffrey Dunn, Fancy Goods Dealer.
8   A. G. Mills & Co. Ltd., Booksellers
Festival Lounge Bar was in Savoy Buildings from 1953 until 1971. It is now part of the night club and casino complex.
Pier Mansions, twelve flats

here is Alhambra Road

Royal Beach Hotel
St. Helen's Mansions, six flats.

St. Helens Parade
3   Christopher Mayhew, Physician & Surgeon.

3 Rev. Lewis Hancock, Methodist.
Rosetrevor Mansions, seven flats.
1 William Ross, Physician & Surgeon.
Albany Beach Mansions, 12 flats
2 Reginald & Ruth Johns, Masseurs.
3 Leslie Thomas, Physician & Surgeon.
10 Olaf Gleeson, Physician & Surgeon.
Beach Mansions, five flats

here is Granada Road

11 Beach Tower Hotel, Mr. & Mrs. D. Wilson-Mather
13 William Martin, Consulting Surgeon.
20 Robert & William Lytle, Physicians.
22 Rev. Walter Dennis, Vicar of St. Simon's Church.

South Side

Rock Gardens

"The Southsea Rock Gardens were developed in 1932-1933 during the years of the depression, it was a time when the government of the day provided loans and grants to local authorities for schemes which would provide work for the unemployed. The Parks Superintendent at that time was a Mr. Baker. He had a particularly good foreman, Mr. George Pratt, who was a very well known local character and who died a few years ago. (I knew him well because he actually worked for me in the 1960s). With a large number of mainly unskilled men, the massive task was performed which transformed this area of Southsea. This particular area was vulnerable to damage by the sea, was covered with gorse, and often flooded but the construction of the promenade did much to prevent flooding but the salt spray was always a problem.

Work commenced by setting out the area in an informal manner so that straight lines were avoided, the idea was to provide an area of interest not just by using alpines and rock garden plants but by planting colourful annuals in informal patches. It was essential to plant suitable plants immediately alongside the promenade. These plants had to be salt lovers and capable of surviving strong salt laden winds and much of the original planting remains today. In order to enable the plants to develop, wattle fencing was put in place as a barrier, this reduced the velocity of the winds and gradually the plants became strong and thick enough to survive.

Rock Gardens

Hundreds of tons of rock was imported directly from Cumberland and the huge chunks were manhandled and the layout gradually established. Planting commenced with mainly evergreen shrubs, a few herbaceous plants and lots of annuals. This attraction was quickly appreciated by thousands of local people and holiday makers.

After the war, the city made plans to recover from those awful days and Ernest Studley, who preferred to be called John, was appointed Parks Superintendent and he was with the Borough Engineers Department. John soon set about the restoration of Southsea. The Rock Gardens was the first area to be reformed and a massive exercise was undertaken to renovate the entire area which was completely overgrown. Rocks were lifted and replaced and changes were made to the design but John was a marvellous plantsman and as plants became more available he undertook the replanting which was in the main done by George Moulds, the new foreman at Southsea and Ernest Flowers. Specific areas were dedicated to alpines but the greatest skill was in the manner of planting a skeleton of evergreens, many of which are tolerant to marine conditions, but at the same time they were planted to enhance the overall scene.

In 1949, just as the transformation was nearing completion, the rock garden flooded during one of the worst storms ever to effect Southsea, this was due to low barometric pressure and a high tide. The fire service pumped the rock garden dry again very quickly and calculated they removed over a million gallons of salt water. The resulting damage was not so bad as one would have imagined and all dead plants were quickly replanted. The rock gardens was then saturated with water by the staff in an attempt to reduce the salt content of the soil but as a long period of heavy rain pursued, so the salt was percolated through the soil.

In the early 1950s, lighting was installed including lights which changed colour on the fountain, model squirrels with internal lights jumped from tree to tree, and model rabbits with internal lights appeared to jump from place to place disappearing in the shrubs. The idea was to provide enjoyment to local residents and to increase the number of visitors to the city. John was never very keen on the tatty side of these illuminations but favoured the coloured lighting tubes which enhanced the main areas of shrub planting. At the same time two aviaries were introduced and these housed budgies, and canaries at one end and pigeons at the other.

I worked in the Rock Gardens as an apprentice under Ernie Flowers with a colleague apprentice, Michael Vaux, under the foremanship of George Moulds, who later became a very great personal friend of mine until his death about ten years ago. I was working in the Rock Gardens from 1955 until early 1956 and because I was an apprentice I was transferred to other various sections of the department so I could gain an overall knowledge. Working in the Rock Gardens in those days was a very happy experience. It is difficult to realise that at that time Southsea Castle was a no go area completely surrounded by walling and our little Park's yard was immediately alongside Castle Buildings with our accommodation consisting of two large huts!"

Brian Kidd

The Pavilion was planned in 1947 at a proposed cost of £13,873.

"At the eastern end was a cage with rabbits and guinea pigs, while at the western end was another cage with budgerigars. The flower beds were floodlit in the evenings and in the trees illuminated squirrels would jump from branch to branch, illuminated rabbits and other animals lurked in the bushes. The fountain would play sequences of water and was also illuminated. There were other illuminations on the Rock Gardens Pavilion, and the cafes on the seafront. These included by the pier, seals who appeared to throw a coloured ball to each other, a clown with performing dogs, a diver who launched from the board into the sea, cats, dogs, butterflies and a peacock."

"To the west of the pier was for many years a compound where you could see wooden clinker built boats all varnished and ready for the Southsea Sea Anglers. Also near here you could hire a Pedalo – a sea going pedal boat in either blue, red, green or yellow."

South Parade Pier

The original pier was built in 1879 at cost of £9,000. It was opened on 26 July 1879 by Princess Edward of Saxe-Weimar wife of the Governor of Portsmouth. On 19 July 1904 it was burnt down. The remains were bought by the Corporation in 1906. The new pier was opened by the Mayor on 12 August 1908. It cost £70,000 and was 500 feet long, 70 feet wide at the narrowest part, 145 feet at the widest.

Behind the entrance was a skating rink or small concert hall 72 feet square with a single arched roof 29 feet high, maple floored. Then came the Kursaal or pavilion 52 feet by 12 feet and concert pavilion 100 feet by 70 feet height 40 feet, the proscenium was 25 feet 6 inches wide, with a stage 40 feet 6 inches wide 24 feet deep, and the hall could seat 1,100 plus 600 in balcony. In 1933 the stage was enlarged and the old proscenium replaced.

In 1974 the pavilion and main building burnt down during the filming of 'Tommy' by Ken Russell.

The new structure was built in 1975 at cost of £600,000.

In April 1996 it was sold to First Leisure for £1m from City Council and Crown Estate

The front accommodated South Parade Pier Restaurant, Southdown Motor Services, Shawe Hume Ltd., Tobacconists, Mills & Co., Booksellers in the forties.

"In 1925 a gypsy on Epsom Downs told my father that she could see him surrounded by water with thousands of pounds passing through his hands! He visualised a future of opulence sailing around the world in his own yacht.

In 1926 he was appointed Box Office Clerk on South Parade Pier, the gypsy's vision of the future had come true, but not in the way my father had hoped for. He was on a pier not a yacht and the money he handled was not his own. I was three years old at the time, and for the next thirty years, apart from the war, the pier played a very important part in my life.

Many memories come flooding back of those early days. The carnival nights and firework displays, confetti and dancing around the deck bandstand. Jan Ralfini and his band, Younkman, the Tit Bits competitions, Schneider Trophy races, with hundreds of thousands of spectators watching from the beach. The Johnny Walker Test Score Board, Amy Johnson's flying visit, the Fol De Rols with Leonard Henry and those wonderful Sunday Band Concerts in the theatre. Jack Hylton, Ambrose, Geraldo, Jack Payne and many more. Front stalls 3/6d, standing round the balcony 1/-. There were many personalties in those days. Robson the pier manager – I don't think I ever saw him without his top hat ... a big shiny black one and whiter than white gloves.

However of all the characters, I remember most of all Jack Pinnegar the deck foreman and the essence of the pier itself. An ex-navy man big in build, with a large stentorian voice. He ruled with a rod of iron and yet was idolised by all his staff. His only failing was to get a bit confused when the summer hotted up.

Boat traffic was heavy in those days, Sandown, Shanklin, Ventnor, Round the Island, Harbour Trips, hourly boats to Ryde, Cowes and trips up the Beaulieu River. Sometimes there would be two or three or four boats waiting at a time, with queues going in all directions. Once, the Paddle Steamer came in to the wrong landing stage and Jack's queue was facing in the opposite direction. Out came his megaphone and his instructions issued forth. "All you people over there turn round and walk backward." Needless to say confusion reigned. On another occasion – Cowes firework night – there were eager passengers queuing to board the Paddle boats, and smaller boats were sailing to see the fireworks. Jack had to sort them out and again produced the megaphone. "I want all the little Cowes to queue up here and all the big Cowes over there!"

There was also the time when the Kneller School of Music Band was playing the theatre. Jack came rushing up to my father who by then had become manager, and complained bitterly about the advertising. "Its all wrong mixing business with politics" he said. "That poster at the front .. The Kneller School of Music, Every man a socialist." My father gently pointed out that what it actually said was "Every man a soloist!"

It was said that when Jack retired, the pier would close down, such was his personality and involvement in all the pier's affairs. Inevitably, in 1940, his day of retirement came and a memorable retirement party and presentation was held in the morning so Jack could say his farewell. In the afternoon, without any warning the Army arrived, cut the pier in two and closed it down.

The prophesy had come true. Happily six weeks later it reopened.

At that time I was a young junior in the City Treasurers department. First at the Guildhall and after the fire at the Northern Grammar School, in Mayfield Road. By then the war was causing staff problems and I used to help out in the pier box office of an evening. There was dancing in the minor hall to Wally Fry and his Collegians. We used to get two to three hundred people a night ... eight hundred on a Saturday. Admission was 6d. After a busy Saturday night, with a full house, I used to cash up the princely sum of £20.

When the air raids became intense, everyone would take shelter in the ladies cloakroom under the Pier. It was the largest and safest place to be. The band would come down and more often than not a sing song would ensue. With the all clear, it was a case of walking home through the fires and rubble after another night of destruction.

After the Sunday night band concerts the musicians would often gather in the bar at the end of the pier for a party and there were many enjoyable occasions. Just before the war my mother started a Cub Pack at the old Elm Grove Baptist Church .. one of the poorest areas in Portsmouth at that time, and one Sunday night with Billy Cotton, the band leader, at the bar after the show this came up in conversation. Billy said "My dear, go out tomorrow and buy them all uniforms and send the bill to me." A wonderful gesture from a lovely person.

The most sociable band was the Squadronaires with Sgt. Jimmy Miller. The bar parties were so hectic, they all swore it cost them money whenever they played the pier.

Soon after the war started I joined the R.A.F. and for four long years I was parted from my beloved pier. In 1946 when I came home, I made my decision to forego a life of accountancy for the more attractive world of entertainment and started as my father had in the pier box office. Those were the days of returning servicemen with gratuities and long pent up yearning for enjoyment. The pier became the Mecca for entertainment in Portsmouth and the box office was busy from early morning to late at night. In summer boat trips, turnstiles, deckchairs, bars and cafes were busy all day long. Dancing in the pier's minor hall sold out with 800 every night. The summer shows starring such names as Harry Secombe, Peter Sellers, Bob Monkhouse and Derek Roy showed full house notices every night and the money rolled in. It was the pier's golden age.

The stage manager at that time was Bill Brewington. He was another character who spent most of his life on the pier. Somewhere, backstage, he had his own personal hole to the water below, through which he put his nets and produced a constant supply of lobsters. Some nights he would catch six or seven to the delight and pleasure of artistes and staff alike to whom he happily dispensed his catch. His wife, Edie, was in charge of the theatre usherettes and programme sellers and also ran the balcony bar during and after the performances. She was a wonderful lady and was treated as the mother of the pier. She listened to everyone's troubles and went out of her way to help anyone with a problem despite long hours and hard work, she always had a smile on her face and time for everyone.

For a long time the bar manager was a small, quiet, inoffensive man called Freddie Popplewell. One couldn't imagine a more unlikely personality for such a public profession. Nevertheless, he ran his little empire impeccably and rarely was there any trouble. All his life he idolised Evelyn Laye and had attended every first night she had appeared in, no matter where it was. When she was booked to appear on the pier, he asked to be allowed to decorate her dressing room. It took him two days and when finished it was a magnificent sight, full of flowers and arrangements fit for a queen. When Miss Laye saw it, she asked to meet the person who had provided such a spectacle. Freddie was duly introduced and was so overcome by the experience he was unable to say a word. He stood there in front of his idol completely speechless and finally had to leave overcome by emotion.

I can remember vividly the 1953 Coronation Review of the Fleet, when every available boat was put into service to satisfy public demand. In three days we put 32,000 people on boats, taking £16,000 – enormous sums of money for those days.

By then David Evans was the manager and my father had risen to the post of Director. Eventually in 1957 I moved on to further my career, although on every available opportunity I returned to renew old memories. However, after the tragic fire and the re-building of the 'imitation' pier, the love affair faltered and the present pier does not appeal as it used to. But then nothing does as one gets older."

Keith Kinnear

"Back in 1955 there were band concerts in the pavilion of South Parade Pier. It was a popular event for a Sunday evening.

I took my girlfriend, Sheila, to impress her. We stood in the balcony because I was poor. One week it was the band of Sid Phillips and another time it was his brother Woolf. Tito Burns came before he became a booking agent. Harry Gold and his Pieces of Eight came with Sam Costa. Sam was a radio comedian then from Much Binding In The Marsh. But he'd been a band singer. A newer leader came one week, Jack Parnell. He was a drummer with Ted

Heath before. I'd seen Ted Heath and his band a few years before in the Savoy across from the pier. It was very popular with singers, Dickie Valentine, Lita Rosa and Dennis Lotis. George Turner the manager (of the Savoy) booked the Beatles later before they became very famous. An assistant of his part-time was Tom Bates. I knew him a long time ago when he worked in Pinks, Milton Road. He ended as the manager after starting as an errand boy. Mick Mulligan and his Magnolias were more jazz inclined. Their singer was George Melly, an amusing man with smart suits, happily still with us. He has written three books about his life. I managed to find one which amused me very much. So much that I wrote to thank him, through Channel Four. I was surprised to receive a humorous answer. He'd been to Portsmouth as a sailor."

Anton Cox

"To get to the Isle of Wight you could go to the Hard but boats also sailed from Clarence or South Parade Pier. The paddle steamers seemed to take forever to get to the Isle of Wight. On one occasion we set off from South Parade Pier into fog and after a few hours arrived back at South Parade Pier without even a glimpse of the Isle of Wight – no radars then!"

"On the east side of South Parade Pier was a white wooden fenced in area with open air bench seats where we went to watch marionette shows."

"Standing facing South Parade Pier to the left, just off the promenade were a row of kiosks where you could buy refreshments etc., not as they are now but smaller. One, which I remember was kept by a very nice German lady. Here you could buy Horlicks, coffee or tea and hot pies, until quite late at night which was great after swimming.

Along there too were three free enclosures for undressing, one for ladies and girls, one for boys and one for men. In the ladies was a shower all free!

On the same side of the pier was a raft, and it was a great incentive to swim to, and a great achievement. There was also a long board on wheels, to which the speedboats came into, and it was exciting to have a trip in one of these, and get wet through.

On the pier were dances Wednesday evenings, for one shilling, and after 10 o'clock were fireworks.

On the right hand side of the pier were often fishermen, sorting their catch, further onto the Ladies' Mile was the bandstand where quite often there was a dance band and lovely dancing round the bandstand, and it was lovely to go dancing, have a swim and then have deck chairs, chocolate or Horlicks. Many

South Parade Pier

lovely evenings we spent chatting, singing and there were no troubles or rudeness etc."

Between South Parade Promenade and St. Helens Parade are the D Day Memorial Gardens

"The whole of the city was defended against invasion and when I was a little boy, it was not possible to walk on the promenade at all. There were huge concrete blocks and barricades of barbed wire which made access to the beach completely impossible and as a reminder of course we can see one of the huge stones in the D Day Memorial Garden close to South Parade Pier. The great block was just one taken from the promenade as a reminder of the way in which the city was defended during the Second World War."

Brian Kidd

Returning to the promenade

Then came the coach offices:
The Bull's Head Parlour Coaches (E. Byng & Sons)
1923 72 Belgrave Street, 1934-1946 74-86 Belgrave Street.
By 1948 was Byngs Coaches and from 1958-1971 they were

at 291 Fratton Road. In the seventies the garage was moved to Milton. The firm was taken over by Hellyer's of Portchester.

Triumph Safety Coaches (J. Wyatt)

1934-1940 the garage was in Rosetta Road. In 1947 the business was acquired by Hants. & Sussex who sold it to Southdown in 1957 although the firm traded as Triumph Coaches until the early seventies.

Don Motor Coaches (J. Marshall)

1934-1962 28 Bristol Road was the office, the garage was in Ranelagh Road. The garage moved to Rodney Road by 1964

City of Portsmouth South Parade Tea House.

White Heather Motor Service

Founded in the 1920s. 1934-1948 listed at 8 The Retreat. In December 1948 the name was changed to White Heather Transport. From 1953-1976 the office was at 62 Elm Grove and the garage at Richmond Road. In 1977 the firm was taken into B. S. Williams (Hants. & Sussex) as White Heather Travel Ltd.

"The local coach firms all competed for business with day, afternoon and evening tours. The drivers would be lined up enticing you to go on their trip. We often went on the evening mystery tours – normally a trip over the South Downs to Stoner Hill and area with a stop at a country pub. Quite often we would meet my grandparents in the pub, they had been on a different trip with another company but they all used the same pubs."

"Another novel form of transport arrived at Eastney when the first hovercraft ran a service from Eastney to the Isle of Wight. The hovercraft just came up onto the beach and pebbles flew everywhere. Later the company moved to alongside Clarence Pier and had a concrete apron laid. If we went to the beach we always went to Eastney, Mum thought it was cleaner and safer. Her sister and her had been nearly swept away from Clarence Beach one day with the wash from the Queen Mary as it sailed through the Solent. Mum would hire a deck chair for the afternoon, my sister and I would sit on towels on the pebbles."

Southsea Terrace

A terrace of 11 blocks of flats dating from 1842 when they were known as Marine Terrace, the date can be seen on the pipework.

9   (Flat 45) Murray Stuart, Dermatologist

11   (Flat 50) Robert MacKeown, Physician & Surgeon
Castleton Court a post war block of flats designed by Cyril Jolliffe.
        Porthole windows were his trade mark.
16   Merton's Hotel
            In 1867 is shown as Belle Vue House, the house of the Chief
            Brewer of Long's Brewery. It became Merton's Hotel by 1935
            and a pub by 1946. It is currently known as Langtrees.
55   Clarence House first inhabited in 1813.
            Half the arch has disappeared into the later addition of the
            restaurant.
On the corner is the birthplace of one of the most famous comic actors of
recent years. Peg Sellers was appearing in her mother's revue in Southsea at
the King's Theatre. She kept on until her husband Bill left his drums nearby
and took her home. This was to Castle Road where Doctor Little delivered her
son. He was christened Richard but to the world he was Peter – why is a
mystery. Peter was on the stage two weeks later with his mother, father and
Dick Henderson Senior. The applause made him cry that day but he made
millions laugh later. A plaque may be seen on his birthplace to mark 8th
September 1925.

Western Parade

1   Carlton Hotel, C. Mutty
            This was taken over during the war and became Council
            Offices. When the new Civic Offices were built the building
            became flats.
3-4   Mayfair Hotel, Sievers & Hickman
9   George & Mrs. Violet Ross, Physician & Surgeon
10   Wilfred Colwell, Private Hotel
11   Mrs. Annie Guthridge, Private Hotel
13   Cecil Mansions, nine flats
17-18 Trevose Private Hotel, Mrs. Ennew
19-20 Alberta Family & Commercial Hotel
21   Exeter Private Hotel, Mrs. Dunnett
26-27 Gwalia Guest House, Mrs. J. Evans
28-29 Congress House, Mrs. M. Foreman
Grosvenor Hotel
            The site of the Grosvenor is first mentioned in 1780 as the Five
            Cricketers a name which the pub retained in the 1830 listing.
            From 1844 to 1851 the directories refer to the premises as just

the Cricketers. In 1859 as the Five Cricketers Tavern, 1863 just Cricketers again. From 1865 to 1874 back to the Five Cricketers. The address over these years is Southsea Common or Castle Road. In the 1887 directory the name is first given as the Grosvenor Hotel at Emanuel Road, and from 1898 to 1940 Western Parade. The building was rebuilt to designs of local architect A. E. Cogswell in 1903. It was taken over in the war following the bombing of the Sailor's Rest and then in 1946 was converted into flats. It was a Pike's brewery house.

This booklet was compiled by the members of the W.E.A. Local History Group which meets at the North End Adult Learning Centre, Derby Road, North End, Portsmouth. The group is made up of local people who wish to record the history of ordinary peoples' lives and the streets in which they live. The group is very informal and welcomes new members who care to come to Derby Road on a Tuesday evening or write to us.

Current Class Members:
Anton Cox, Frank Deacon, Peter Galvin, Malcolm Garlick *(Chairman)*, Ann Gilbert, Kevin Goldring, Stephen Pomeroy *(Editor)*, Chris Redgrave, Brad Smith, Jeff Smith, Rita Wall, Margaret Webster *(Treasurer)*

Honorary Members:
Don Miles *(Typesetting)*.

Affiliated Members:
Des Beaumont, Morecambe, Lancashire

Contributors:
Mrs. Dorothy Aslett, Alan Keel, Brian Kidd, Keith Kinnear, Mrs. Williams *(nee Bone)*

Illustrations:
Cover	Based on Postcard produced by F. Alexander, London.
Castle Buildings	Postcard by local company Hayling Island Photographic.
Canoe Lake	Postcard by local company John Welch & Sons.
Clarence Parade	Postcard – no publishers details given.
Rock Gardens	Postcard by John Valentine & Sons, Dundee. Attempts have been made to contact Valentines regarding copyright but without success.
South Parade Pier	J. Welch & Sons, Portsmouth.

References:	Kelly's Directories, B.M.A. Conference Handbook, Council Records, Portsmouth City Museum & Records Office - W. Tarring Papers.

FIRST PUBLISHED IN 2000.
Copyright on all materials in this booklet remains with the contributors and the W.E.A.